Dedication:
For no one in particular.

Table of Contents:

SIMPLE POTIONS

TEA MAGIC

TEA BLEND POTION RECIPES

STORM MAGIC

SEASONAL MAGIC

GROUNDING METHODS

SPELLS

LOVE SPELLS

FRIENDSHIP SPELLS

GLAMOURS

PROTECTION SPELLS

BINDINGS

COMMUNICATION SPELLS

CURSES

So You Just Picked This Book Up

Witchcraft is one of those things it's a bit hard to find advice on, as it is a bit strange in our times to go around asking people if they are witches. Even google is not helpful if you don't know the questions to ask, which can often be the case when stumbling upon something new where everyone else seems to already be in the know. So here are a few questions and answers in case you needed either of them.

Do you cast spells and stuff? Does anything happen when you do? What is the general thing witches do?

Yes, witches cast spells. That's the main thing, but there's also a lot of other things we do. Sometimes things happen, sometimes things don't. Magic can be hit or miss.

Is it real?

I can no more tell you that witchcraft is real than tell you that gods are real. It's something every witch has to decide for themselves. Personally, to me, witchcraft is real, and so I practice my craft.

Do you believe in ghosts? What about aliens? Maybe one but not the other. Sometimes, it's just fun to believe, sometimes, it helps deal with the unexplained, sometimes it is even believed just for the sake of helping someone get through some tough times. Either way, what you believe is up to you. But if you want it to be real, it is.

Is it mostly about being closer to nature?

The point of witchcraft is different for all of us, I think. Being closer to nature is some of it, for some of us. However, some choose not to include nature in their craft, much to the judgement of traditionalist witches.

My mom says it's evil and while I don't really believe that I was wondering if you could give insight into it?

Witchcraft is only as evil or good as the person who uses it. And really, most people don't fall into labels as simple as "good" or "evil".

How many branches of witchcraft are there? Can you go into any branch? And how do you choose your branch?

Infinite! Any one you choose! However many as you want! You go into whatever you like! You don't have to stay there if you lose interest either, there are very few instances witchcraft will demand you make a lifelong commitment.

Branches of witchcraft tend to be very open ended. Do as you like, but take care to not steal from closed cultures, and learn where the boundaries of what is off limits is, such as voodoo, Santeria, and various other things that qualify as cultural appropriation.

What's the difference between a grimoire and a Book of Shadows?

A grimoire is a general book of spells, a book of shadows is a Wiccan term. Originally, a Book of shadows, sometimes called a BoS, is a collection of ritual texts and guidelines that are used in the Gardnerian Tradition.

Witchcraft Basics

To Be a Witch" Falsehoods

There are a lot of misconceptions lately in the community on what someone needs to be a witch, I would like to clear some up.

YOU DO NOT NEED:

FANCY TOOLS –

Or any tools at all, really. All you need is yourself and your intent. Sure, tools that fit your aesthetic are nice, but you don't need them to do magic. If you have the ability to buy them and you want to, there's no one stopping you, but *please* don't feel like you have to go out and buy yourself an etsy broom or a cauldron. Don't stress yourself out over making one either! They are but trappings.

APPEARANCE –

In witchy aesthetic photos, it's usually a slim, white girl with long hair. That lack of a more diverse representation can give the impression that you need to look and be a certain way, but please know it is untrue. It does not matter what your race, weight, hair, or anything looks like.

AESTHETIC –

You don't need to dress "like a witch". A witch can look like anything. If you want to indulge in the "black hat, black clothes" look, fine, but you don't need to confine yourself to it if it's not your thing. You can look like whatever you want to. Wear pink! And ruffles! Or a t-shirt and jeans is just fine. Whatever you are comfortable in.

GENDER –

There are some in the community that will fight tooth and nail to make it seem you have to be a cisgender female to call yourself a witch. Anyone can be a witch, regardless of gender. Female, male, non-binary, agender, trans, demi, etc.

BLACK CAT –

You don't need a black cat. You don't need to have a familiar either, though I understand there is a great pressure to have one. Those are unique relations that should not be forced to happen.

A DARK, MYSTICAL ATTITUDE –

You don't need to suddenly start talking like Chaucer or put effort into having an air of mystery. You don't need to be holier than thou, or act like you know it all. Witchcraft is a journey that takes time to learn.

CURSING –

No, you don't need to curse, many witches don't. But you don't need to shame someone for cursing either, that is rude, and forcing your beliefs on others.

ON A SPIRITUAL PATH –

Witchcraft does not have to be spiritual! You can practice magic without having to worry about being "spiritual enough", because each craft is unique and deeply personal, you don't need to force it to be something that you're not invested in.

INVESTED IN NATURE –

Some witches will insist magic can only come from nature. They are simply wrong. Magic comes from you, the witch. The tools you use, whether plants or plastic, do not alter this fact.

RELIGIOUS –

There are many witches that wonder where the power comes from if they don't call upon a god. The power can come from you. You do not need to devote yourself to a god. Devoting is a highly dedicated and involved commitment, and should be taken seriously as one would a marriage.

WICCAN –

Wicca is not the only way to do witchcraft, it is only one way of practicing magic. There are many people who think the only way to do witchcraft is to be Wiccan, but they are misinformed. If you do not want to work with Wiccan influences or traditions, you do not have to.

FOLLOWING THE REDE-

The Wiccan Rede, the threefold law, it has a lot of names. It is the belief that whatever energy you emit, will visit your three times over. If you are not Wiccan, you do not have to follow this rule.

INITIATED –

Some practices, some traditions, initiation is needed. However, to be a witch in general, you don't need to go through any ritual to prove yourself one. Be wary of those who insist you do, they are often trying to take advantage of new witches.

STRAIGHT / CIS –

Some traditions you'll encounter have homophobic roots/influences. While it is discouraging, you don't have to listen to those, or you can work with others to rework phobic traditions.

A "NATURAL" WITCH –

Some people will claim to have "witch's blood" or "the flame", meaning witchcraft has been in their families for generations. This does not make them superior or more of a witch than you. Anyone who wants to be a witch can, no matter their birth circumstances.

LABELLED –

A lot of witches label their craft, "herb witch", "space witch", "storm witch" etc. You can be as many as you want, or none if it pleases you. You do not need to label your craft However, some people can't put their craft in a box, and are referred to as eclectic.

WHAT YOU NEED IN ORDER TO BE A WITCH:

The simple desire to be a witch, the intent to cast spells, and to practice the craft in which it appears to you, to the best of your ability and creativity.

Other Witches and You

There are many other witches in the world, and no two witches' crafts are exactly alike. Here are some common themes/traditions that you can choose whether or not to incorporate into your craft

THREEFOLD LAW/WICCAN REDE –
A lot of people don't realize that if you're not Wiccan, you don't have to follow this. Some non-wiccans do follow it. it's a nice philosophy, to not harm anyone, but like every philosophy, it is not a mandatory way of thinking

DON'T CURSE –
Goes in hand with the rede, some witches are very adamant about not cursing. And that is their choice! But they don't get a say in whether or not you get to curse, or whether or not you should. You have your reasons, and they have theirs.

INITIATION ONLY –
If you choose to go through one, all the power to you. Initiation can really help some witches become confident in their abilities, and others feel they are a witch from day one. However, no one can tell you you're not a true witch because you're not initiated in any traditions.

TUTORED –
A traditionalist notion among some witches is that being an apprentice to another witch with more experience than you is necessary. It can be cool to have a mentor, but there are mentors that abuse that power. a mentor can only teach you the craft as they have perceived it, and you are welcome to learn it that way, but know if you don't want a

mentor you can become a witch by teaching yourself, as many do.

LOVE AND LIGHT –
   A lot of witches say this constantly, and it can get a bit awkward if you didn't turn to witchcraft for those reasons. Witchcraft can be about good things and positivity, but it can also be about revenge, curses, and protecting oneself. Both are valid approaches to witchcraft.

IN A COVEN –
   Though it's not as common as it used to be, being a solitary witch was once a built it community of witches can be a great thing to have, but it isn't for everyone.

CLEANSE/GROUND/CAST CIRCLE FOR EVERY SPELL -
Though you may use a spell someone else wrote, casting circles and constant cleansing and grounding isn't necessary for every witch. Some witches it must be done, but others it's just something you might do.

EMOJI SPELLS –
   No one is forcing you to use them, you don't have to if you don't think they actually work. But if they work for you, use them all you want! if you can find the magic in something unconventional and new, all the power to you.

NATURALIST –
   The typical idea of witchcraft is that it involves old, natural things. Some people choose to only use natural things in their craft because they like the connection to nature, or don't feel that synthetic objects fit into witchcraft.

SYNTHETIC –
   Some witches, particularly tech witches, incorporate a lot of modern technology. Some have a hard time finding the magic in a plastic object. It really depends on you and whether or not you can see things as magical that have not traditionally been interpreted as such or just haven't been around long enough to feel like legitimate magic.

RELIGION –

It can be hard to comprehend where the power behind a spell is if a god hasn't blessed it for some witches. But if you don't feel connected to a god, or aren't uplifted by your religion, you don't need to force yourself to find one. Witchcraft it plenty powerful without religion.

WHAT YOU CAN'T PICK AND CHOOSE:

- ❖ smudging
- ❖ karma/chakras
- ❖ spirit animals
- ❖ voodoo/Santeria
- ❖ general cultural appropriative stuff
- ❖ stuff from closed cultures

Remember! Your craft if yours, his craft is his, her craft is hers, their craft is theirs. None of them have to follow any of the other's traditions, and no one should force or pressure someone else into incorporating certain aspects in their

If anyone ever tells you, "You MUST do it this way" take a moment and figure out if it agrees with your path or not.

Religion and the Witch

A common misconception you will come across by many witches themselves is that witchcraft is a religion. It is not.

Witchcraft by itself is not a religion, it is a practice that can be incorporated into religions. It is a practice that can stand alone, secularly.

Wicca is a religion that includes witchcraft, not the other way around. Not all wiccans practice witchcraft either.

Almost any religion can be practiced with witchcraft alongside it, as long as the religion does not forbid it. And here is where another common misconception comes in: Christianity dislikes witches.

There are many who do not know this misconception started when King James had his own version of the bible made, with various bits of input and rewording. "Thou shall not suffer a witch to live", and the handful of other phrases he had put into the bible are merely a product of King James' personal fear of witches, and are not original to the bible. So, yes, actually, a witch can practice both the craft and Christianity if they so please, without breaking any rules.

However, there are many other pantheons that witches interact with, as the witchcraft, pagan, and heathen communities tend to have a bit of an overlap. There are Astaru witches (Norse pantheon), Hellenic polytheist witches (Greek pantheon), Kemetic witches (Egyptian pantheon), and many others. The rules and religions often each have their own rules about how to worship and speak to each set of gods.

It is also possible to find divine inspiration from a nameless source, and learn its name from the continued practice. There is the birth of a new god, a new religious practice.

However, to emphatically repeat it, religion is not mandatory to witchcraft. Witchcraft needs nothing but you.

A Word on Wicca

One of the most widespread misconceptions of witchcraft is that all witchcraft is Wicca. Witchcraft existed before Wicca, and has been shaped differently by every culture and place that is has been practiced. It continues to be shaped as we progress and learn new ways we can use it.

Let's separate the idea that there is such a thing as "Wiccan" magic and "non wiccan" magic. Magic is magic. There are some, like wiccans, who practice magic through the lens of their religion. There are others who use magic without bothering with that. Magic can be framed in many different ways and traditions, and restricted by rules of a tradition. It does not need to be used through a religion, but some people prefer the structure and traditions.

Basic Terms to Know

ENERGY MANIPULATION

GROUNDING—
>To ground is an exercise that is used to clear and release excess energy, as well as to renew the energies within oneself and clear out the old.
>Traditionally done by envisioning roots stretching out from oneself into the ground, like a tree, and connecting through them to the earth. However, it can be done with simple visualization, and does not need to include nature, as long as the cycling of energy is completed. Various techniques will be mentioned later.

CENTER—
>Usually done after grounding. To center oneself is to organize and become aware of the energies within you, and overall be magically aware.

CLEANSE—
>To remove negative or unwanted energies, spirits, and imprints from an object or a space. There are a number of simple rituals and actions that are done to cleanse.
>This is often done to rid an object of past memories or uses, to make it spiritually new.

CHARGE—
>To infuse an object with personal or external power/energies/intent. There are vast many methods that can be used to charge an object, water, or crystal.

VISUALIZE—
>Similar to imagining, the intended conjuring of images in one's mind that are accompanied by energy, and used to help conduct one's intent.

INTENT—
>Your goal, or purpose behind casting a spell. The emotions and power within you that power the spell and bring about the effect of the spell.

To CONSECRATE—

The ritual blessing of an object or place by cleansing it and instilling with a specific energy. Cannot be done to living creatures.

SPELL TYPES

SPELL – a manifestation of intents, ingredients, and influences combined to bring about an intangible effect

CURSE—

A spell designed to cause a person or place harm or misfortune of a grand scale. Occasionally used to protect when it used against a concept, "cursing out" infections and medical problems.

HEX—

Commonly thought as similar to a curse, though it comes from a German word for witch. Commonly interpreted as a weaker curse, or a midpoint between a jinx and a curse on a scale of annoying to devastating.

JINX—

A spell to cause momentary bad luck or annoyance, but can occasionally come back to bite someone later. Usually paired with irony, or used to bring about the opposite effect of what someone says out loud or hopes for.

BANISHING—

A type of spell, designed to get rid of something specific, whether it be a concept, a person, spirit, or otherwise, and to keep it away.

WARDING—

A type of protective spell in which you create and put up magical walls, usually against a specific thing, such as spirits or negative people, but could be used for evangelicals and teenagers that theoretically loiter on your lawn.

BINDING—

Similar to banishing. Instead of removing a person, object, or situation from your vicinity, you prevent a person or creature from performing a particular action.

GLAMOUR—
Often used for beauty spells, are a type of spell used for creating an illusion over a person or object. They can be used for a number of purposes, to make someone more attract, or to make an object harder to find, or a person be more or less likely to be noticed.

POTION—
Any drink made to have a magical effect.

JAR SPELL—
A spell made and contained within a jar, often herb sealed with wax.

BEWITCHED OBJECTS

CHARM—
Any object that is worn or used that is meant to have magical effects on the holder/user.

AMULET—
Usually a natural object, worn to ward off illness, evil, and possession. Often crystal-based, for protection.

TALISMAN—
Typically gives power to the wearer, often a crafted object that has gone through a consecration ceremony.

How to Cast a Spell

At first the concept of how to cast a spell can be hard to grasp, because it's not as complete an action as turning on the lights. Even some rituals can feel as though they lack a certain closure, even when they are complete.

However, the simplest way to describe it is to fill something with intent. It's not a solid action and that is why it is somewhat different for every witch, and why it can feel incomplete or not enough, because there's no final button to push. This can be helped with ritual parts added to a spell, blowing out a candle, burying something, burning, etc. Such gestures within a spell can be as important as the energy you summon and shape for the spell.

Filling a spell with intent is something hard to nail down because it's somewhat different for every witch. Some witches rely on the power of herbs and stones to replace intent, but for the most part every witch finds a source of power within themselves and it can be different for everyone. In general I would say, look for emotion, and try to channel that.

Tools of Witchcraft

As you go along your path, you'll find there are many tools used in witchcraft, and they all have different purposes. Not all witches use the same tools; some use unconventional ones, some don't use any. Here are some that are well known.

You do not need to use any or all of them, you do not need to rush out and buy them. Each tool you use should have meaning and importance to you and your practice, and that is not something that can be rushed.

WAND—
For directing energy in rituals and spells. Represents energy, power, and fertility, used as both air and fire element. This can be anything, from a stick, to a pencil, to a spoon.

BROOM / BESOM—
   Air element, for cleansing negative energy out of a space, or to clear the way for a different type of energy. There are many different ways to make a besom, but any old broom will do.

CHALICE —
   For a mixture that does not need heat applied, for offerings of drinks, or a spell you intend to drink. It's a water element that can be any type of cup.

CRYSTALS—
   Earth elementals, often used for conducting and charging and storing specific types of energy. Sometimes the shape can influence how the energy is used.

CANDLES—
   Fire elements good for color magic, also good for applying a fire element. Can be carved, anointed with oils or herbs. They come in a variety of shapes: tea lights, votive, pillar, taper and jar candles. Some scented candles can be used instead of incense.

CAULDRON—
   Water elements for mixing, cooking, and burning things. Heat resistant. Does not need to be the typical idea of a cauldron, it can be any fire/heatproof pot or kettle.

ATHAME—
   Though often characterized as a "black blade", an athame can be any knife you set aside for cutting up plants, or harvesting herbs. Like a wand, it can be used in rituals to direct energy in a more hostile manner. Considered a fire element

BELL—
   Air element, for cleansing and clearing out, and bringing new energies in, very similar to a broom. For calling and dispelling spirits.

JARS—

Good for containing ingredients, potions (assuming properly kept and sanitized), and herbs, and especially jar spells. Sometimes a jar is the only tool you need in a spell.

Building a Broom/Besom

A witch's broom, or a *besom* is tool used in witchcraft to cleanse spaces or purify an area as ritual preparation. In the middle ages, it was used to apply flying ointment to the body to aid in astral travel, and even used in some hand-fasting ceremonies. It is associated with the air symbol.

BESOMS ARE HIGHLY CUSTOMIZABLE

You can have several different besoms for different occasions and purposes. The materials you use to build one can have an impact on what magics you use it for.
A traditional wiccan besom is made from a hawthorn staff with birch twig bristles, tied together using willow. However, your broom can be made of anything you like.

If you are going to be using straw, soak the straw in water for a few hours to make it more pliable. It will be less likely to snap and easier to weave in a pattern, if you so choose.

THE STAFF

A few possibilities for staff handles based on wood magic correspondences:

ALDER—
Weather magic, necromancy, courage and passion

ALMOND—
Wisdom, prosperity, love magic, healing

BIRCH—
Intuition, creativity, love, healing, protection

ELDER—
Healing, protection, banishment

HAZEL—
Truth, divination

HOLLY—
Purity, sun magic, strength, protection, luck

OAK—
Protection, fertility, strength

REDWOOD—
"King of trees", strength, protection, creativity, enlightenment

ROWAN—
Defense, creation, travel

WILLOW—
Healing, protection, spirit work

YEW—
Strength, change

THE BRISTLES

You can use twigs of any of kind of tree, which will have its own correspondences.

DRIED HERBS—
Lavender, sage, rosemary, baby's breath, etc

DRIED FLOWERS—
Marigold, roses, lilac, etc.

BIRD FEATHER—
   Corresponds to the type of bird, or simply air element if an assortment of feathers.

IMBUNED POWERS

   You can soak the besom in a tea bath to allow it to take on new abilities.

WHITE TEA—
   Air magic, purification, protection, clarity, realization, meditation, cleansing

GREEN TEA—
   Fire magic, healing, love, catalysts, mindfulness, passion, sexual health and new energies

BLACK TEA—
   Strength, stability, endings, finished business, and banishment, expelling negativity.

FRUIT, HERBAL, OR FLORAL TEAS will correspond to the meanings of those fruits, strawberry for love, lemon for cleansing, etc.

ASSEMBLY
   Gather your staff, bristles, and binding method of choice. You can either:

❖ bind the bristles together and stab/push the staff into the center of them
❖ bind the bristles around the staff
❖ bind the bristles around the staff so the ends are in the middle, and fold them down so they face the correct direction, and bind again around them

OTHER CUSTOMIZATIONS:
❖ runes/sigils can be carved into the staff handle
❖ knot magic - weave the bristles

- ❖ ribbons and color magic
- ❖ various stones and gems can be embedded
- ❖ tie flowers and plants to it

A Witch's Wand

In witchcraft, a wand is used for directing energy in rituals and spells. It represents energy, power, and fertility, and is used as both air and fire element. Each wand can be as unique as the witch that wields it.

Unlike brooms, wands require very little work put into their production, unless you want to. Some traditions call for a witch to find their wand in a fallen branch and forbid against breaking one off the tree. Carving is optional, as is the choice to embed it with crystals, wrap it with wire, tie with ribbon, carve sigils, etc.

For wood correspondences, please refer to the "staff" section of the broom chapter.

However, please note, a wand does not need to be made out of wood. A wand can be found in many things and anything that is dear to you. A spoon, a pencil, a wrench, a plastic toy wand. If you can find magic within the instrument, it can be a wand.

Candle Magic

In spells candles are often used as a fire element, whether for burning herbs, objects, dripping wax onto something or simply staying lit for a few hours. They are often very useful for color magic, also good for applying a fire element. Can be carved, anointed with oils or herbs. They come in a variety of shapes: tea lights, votive, pillar, taper and jar candles. Some scented candles can be used instead of incense.

RED—
Strength, courage, passionate love, lust, anger. Represents Mars.

ORANGE—
Legal matters, success, vitality, passion, enthusiasm. Represents Saturn.

YELLOW—
Friendship, happiness, communication. Represents the sun.

GREEN—
Healing, money, prosperity, luck, employment, youth. Represents Jupiter.

BLUE—
Healing, sleep, calm, peace, wisdom. Represents Neptune.

PURPLE—
Power, exorcism, astral, psychic abilities, spirituality. Represents mercury.

INDIGO—
Protection, the home, intuition, travel. Represents Uranus.

PINK—
Romantic love, fidelity, truth, gratitude, technology. Represents Venus.

WHITE—
New beginnings, quiet, seriousness. Represents the moon

BLACK—
Elegance, power, absolution. Represents Pluto.

Altars in Witchcraft

An altar can be a work-space where you cast spells and do most of your magic, or it can be a place where you worship gods and leave offerings.

You can put anything you like on it! it really depends on what you are using it for, and try to put things that relate to that purpose.

For example:

A workspace altar might have a cauldron, a place to burn herbs, some stored herbs, candles, a besom (or any witchy tools you might use). An altar would be as unique as your craft, and be all about the things you like to include in your craft.

An altar for worship could have figurines/statuettes of the gods you worship, related or representative objects, etc. for Aphrodite I might put seashells and hearts, for Dionysus, grapes, vines, and if he approves, a party hat even. In general, perhaps a plate where food offerings go, and a cup for drink offerings, and a fire safe place to burn things, maybe even an incense holder.

And of course, you can combine them or find a new purpose for an altar!

Potions Overview

WHAT IS A POTION?

A potion, is any drink made to have a magical effect. From the Latin *potio* and the French *potare*, a poisonous drink. However, as the connotation of the word has changed with popular media, it doesn't have to poison anybody. In fact, let's try not to do that.

TYPES OF POTIONS:

There are many names for potions, and they indicate different methods of creation and application.

INFUSION—
A drink prepared by soaking the leaves of a plant or herb in hot water or alcohol for 5-10 min. to be drunk when cooled

DECOCTION—
An infusion prepared by simmering a tougher substance, such as a bark, for 10-30 minutes. to be drunk.

TINCTURE—
A medicine made by dissolving a herb in alcohol for a week. to be taken sparingly in small amounts

VINEGAR—
Similar to a tincture, but instead of alcohol, vinegar is used. to be added into other foods in small amounts

SYRUP—
Ingredients that are preserved in sugar solution, a reduced infusion/decoction with added sugar. to be taken sparingly in small amounts

POULTICE—
A soft, moist mass of fresh chopped plant material, applied to the body with a cloth.

SAFETY FIRST!

Knowing how the potion is prepared does not necessarily mean it is safe to use or consume, that depends on knowledge of the herbs you're working with, how much of one herb is healthy to ingest, how they interact with other chemicals, and awareness of any allergies you might have to them.

Under no circumstances, is it recommended or legal to put a potions or herbs in someone else's drink/food without their knowledge or consent.

⚠ Please avoid working with toxic or dangerous ingredients unless you have the proper training, for your own safety.

⚠ Ask your doctor about herbs conflicting with any medications you're taking, before consuming herbal potions

⚠ Take extra precautions with herbal ingredients when pregnant or dealing with a medical condition.

The idea of making a potion can be daunting, there are so many factors to get right, the herbs, combinations, potency, the preparation, storing, side effects or drug interactions, etc. however, to potions do not have to be a dangerous or complicated activity.

A potion can be a simple, subtle brew of coffee, tea, hot chocolate, or infused water, with simple, everyday ingredients added that correspond to various uses. These fall under infusions, the simplest type of potion to make, which is in fact what tea is. For beginners, working with ingredients you are familiar with that have not caused you problems before is the best route to take.

When to Cast a Spell - By Weekdays

While casting spells does not have to only happen on the days that are best for it, some witches believe timing to be important for their spells, while others do not care. Here are some correspondences that you can choose to follow, or not.

MONDAY—
Glamours, beauty and confidence spells. Weather work. Healing spells.

TUESDAY—
Communication and love spells, friendship spells. Any delicate magic. Plant and herb-based magic

WEDNESDAY—
Cursing, hexes, bindings and banishments. Space and cosmic witchcraft.

THURSDAY—
Spells for travel and protection, astral travel and psychic protections. Sea witchcraft, hedgecraft.

FRIDAY—
Any spell planned for someone else, love/lust spells. Banishing barriers, friendship spells. Kitchen witchcraft.

SATURDAY—
Job and money spells, success and motivation spells. Creativity and truth.

SUNDAY—
Intuition spells, justice and legality.

When to Cast a Spell - By Time of Day

DAWN—
   Breaking curses, beauty and glamour spells. Weather and sea spells. Magic involving delicate feelings, friendship and forgiveness, budding romance.

MORNING—
   Fertility, good luck, green/herbal witchcraft. Best time to brew potions. Intuition and justice.

NOON—
   Wealth and career spells. Success and motivation. Confidence and courage spells. Kitchen magic.

AFTERNOON—
   The time to gather herbs. Communication spells. Travel protections.

EVENING—
   Psychic protections, peace/balance spells. Kitchen spells and pop culture spells.

TWILIGHT—
   Catalysts, movement and growth. Astral travel and divination. Love/lust spells. Technology witchcraft.

NIGHT—
   Curses, hexes, banishment, bindings. Space and cosmic magic. Dream magic. Hedgecraft.

MIDNIGHT—
   Creativity, switching between realms. Spirit work, liminal spaces, reaching through the veil.

Cleansing

Cleansing is a way of removing negative or unwanted energies, spirits, and imprints from an object or a space. There are a number of simple rituals and actions that are done to cleanse. You can do as many or as few as you like, and create your own cleansing methods/rituals.

CLEANSING ONESELF

- ❖ Brush your hair, morning
- ❖ Ritual baths
- ❖ Dancing singing
- ❖ Visualization
- ❖ Drinking a tea designed to cleanse

DISCREET METHODS

- ❖ Brush your hair
- ❖ Open the windows, let the new air come in and the old air out
- ❖ Light a candle
- ❖ Playing a song you associate with cleansing
- ❖ Ringing wind chimes
- ❖ Wetting your hands in salt water and flicking the water through the area
- ❖ Visualize light and colors, and manipulate the energy away

OPEN AREA METHODS

- ❖ Ring a bell through an area
- ❖ Waft incense smoke around
- ❖ Burn herbs, such as sage, rosemary, bay leaf, etc
- ❖ Spritz lemon-infused water around, or salt water
- ❖ Light a candle
- ❖ Sprinkle salt or eggshell pieces in the windows and doorways
- ❖ Use a besom to clean the negative energies out of the air like cobwebs

- ❖ Wave a branch of a strong-scented herb through the area, such as mint
- ❖ Toss a pinch of salt or herbs in the door ways and window
- ❖ Touch each corner of the room and say a short prayer over each
- ❖ Smoke cleansing / cense (not smudging)

When Your Spell Fails

No witch succeeds with their spells 100% of the time. This a short list of reasons why it could have happened and some solutions.

DISTRACTION—
A spell you're not invested in isn't going to have much power behind it. If you're concentrated more on you. if you cast a motivation spell while planning out your vacation, it's going to subtract from that motivation.

ROSEMARY REPLACES EVERYTHING—
Supposedly. It supplies general power, but if you add nothing into the spell that has any real meaning to you, then what is that power supposed to do? Where does that energy go with no direction?

ASSOCIATIONS—
The correspondences everyone else lists for herbs and stones and planets can be very useful, but sometimes you have a personal conflicting association. Perhaps lavender is gross to you, and not peaceful at all. Then that dream sachet isn't going to give you peaceful dreams.

DIDN'T HELP THE SPELL—
Magic does not exist in a vacuum. Spells can only do so much, but if you don't make the effort, it much less likely to work. Job spells don't work if you don't fill out applications, love spells don't work if you don't go out and talk to people, and so on.

TOO MANY COOKS—

If you cast 10 love spells, and yet no one is attracted to you, it's entirely possible they all did work but they all conflicted with each other, and ended up canceling each other out.

SHOT FOR THE STARS—

Sometimes you try to achieve something, and you set your expectations too high. Either it's impossible, you're trying from the wrong angle, or you didn't get as much as you wanted.

CANCELLATION—

Sometimes a spell may appear not to work when it does, but the results are invisible because it canceled something else out. Say you cast a money spell and get no extra cash after several weeks, it could be just helping you maintain your current income and blocking extraneous expenses.

IMPATIENCE—

Unless you programmed a working time limit into it, the spell could be working and you just don't see the results yet. These things can take time.

OUT OF YOUR DEPTH—

If you don't feel like you're ready to do a spell, your lack of confidence or discomfort can either disable the spell or not give it enough power to work

WHAT TO DO:

❖ Take a break, ground, cleanse, and give it time. refocus your intentions
❖ Contemplate each ingredient and step in the spell, and modify
❖ Use the ingredients that you know best work for you, old standards hold up.
❖ Think about what you could do to help the spell work. What mundane methods haven't you tried?

❖ Take a step back and look at it realistically. is there another angle you can approach this from, can you break it down into smaller steps?
❖ Return to the spells you are comfortable doing, and work from there.

On Writing Your Own Spells

Every craft is unique. Some paths have more structure and ritual in them, like Wicca and ceremonial witchcraft, etc. However, carving a new path for yourself, as many eclectic and secular witches do, you might notice that nearly every step is optional, even casting a circle. That being said, feel free to incorporate as many or as few into each spell you cast.

There isn't really a way to ensure a successful spell from your side of things, the most you can do is trial and error and eventually with practice you'll figure out what works for you. The most you can do is be clear in your intent and respectful of the elements you work with. ALL STEPS ARE OPTIONAL. PICK AND USE WHAT YOU WANT TO.

CHOOSE AN INTENT:

BANISHMENT—
For keeping away negative energy and entities

BEAUTY—
To do with one's looks, for the eye of the beholder or otherwise

COURAGE—
For confidence, mental strength

DIVINATION—
For aid in psychic and clairvoyant abilities

FERTILITY—
For conception, creativity, abundance of life and positive energy

FIDELITY—
    For faithfulness and loyalty.

FOCUS—
    For concentration, motivation, and specifying a purpose

FORTUNE—
    For good luck, careers, wealth, and monetary gain

FRIENDSHIP—
    For bonding

HAPPINESS—
    For general good times and good feelings

HEALING—
    For emotional recovery and rejuvenation

LOVE—
    For romance, platonic love, self love, etc.

MEMORY—
    For improving memory or forgetting

PEACE—
    For ending negative or tumultuous times

PROTECTION—
    For general safety, against physical or spiritual harm

PURIFICATION—
    For cleansing, consecration, removing all energies

TRUTH—
    For honesty, vision through difficult situations

WISDOM—
    For hindsight, clear views on experiences and good judgment

COMMON METHODS OF CASTING SPELLS

TO BIND—
   Wrap in black thread, drip wax over, or seal in a jar and hide it in the dark.

TO BANISH—
   Burn an effect to ash and sweep off the back door step, cast it out a window, or bury in the ground and spit on it

TO ENCOURAGE—
   Plant it by the front door/steps, bury by a window, or place it on a windowsill

TO HIDE—
   Place in a jar painted black, cover with cloth and bury, or wrap with a ribbon

TO CLEANSE—
   Bury it in a bowl of salt, burn herbs and pass through the smoke, or lay it in a moonwater bath

TO GLAMOUR—
   Leave under the full moon, hold its reflection over a mirror with herbs

TO WISH—
   Place before a candle and blow it out, drown a coin in water, or let seeds blow into the wind

TO COMMUNICATE- (with a spirit or deity)—
   Anoint a candle, leave out offerings, or open the front doors and windows

TO WARD—
   Leave part of the spell in four corners, draw lines around the protected area, or plant an object of projection in the north, east, south, and west edges

TO CURSE—

Spit on it, drag your nails down it, or stick sharp things in it

TO DISCOURAGE—
Plant or bury by the back door, or burn to ash

TO JINX—
Say it three times out loud, or say a word the same time as someone else

TO MANIPULATE—
Use wax, use poppets, or tie several strings to pieces of an effect

TO BENEFIT—
Light a candle, charge a crystal, or create a talisman

PREPARATION:

- ❖ Research herbs, crystals and materials by correspondences
- ❖ Deities, spirits or beings to invoke
- ❖ What tools you're going to use

PRECAUTIONS:

- ❖ Cleanse the area/workspace/tools
- ❖ Charge tools/ingredients with intent
- ❖ Waiting for/choosing a time of day/week/planet influence/zodiac sign/ lunar cycle most appropriate
- ❖ Grounding/meditation
- ❖ Casting a circle
- ❖ Call up any spirits/deities you're going to work with

CASTING:

- ❖ give offering to spirits/deities
- ❖ light candles
- ❖ say the chant
- ❖ put stuff together/burn stuff
- ❖ bury/bottle the ingredients and store it somewhere safe

CLEANUP:

- ❖ thank and send away the spirits/deities
- ❖ cleanse the area/tools used
- ❖ call down the circle
- ❖ grounding/meditation

It's more about what you want to include, and there's no set structure. You can even invent your own steps. Some days you'll have more time to include more steps, some spells might even feel like they should be more complicated.

Common Sense and Witchcraft

Witchcraft and the Law

There are just some things that are against the law, and practicing witchcraft does not make one allowed to simply do as they please. This isn't aimed at your religious freedoms, this is about following the laws of the land you live in. While your religion/spiritual beliefs may allow and encourage it, that may not be coincide with what is legal in your area.

This is a gathered collection of things based on my experience in America and in reference to American law.

BIRD FEATHERS –

Some species of birds and animals are endangered and collecting their feathers or remains is against the law. This varies from state to state, so you should check the laws of your area before collecting things you find in the wild.

PLANTS/ANIMAL PARTS IN THE MAIL –

There are a number of restrictions on what can and cannot be safely mailed in a sanitary method, and they need to be followed.

TEACHING WITCHCRAFT TO MINORS –

In many places, it is the parents who get first and only say in what religion is taught to their child, until they reach the age of majority. Legal action can often be brought against those who teach a minor witchcraft without the parent's consent.

DIGGING UP BONES –

Just no. collecting bones that somehow come out of the graves is off the table too. The selling and buying and overall collection of human bones is often illegal, if not entirely.

LITTERING –
     Spells that tell you to bury a glass jar somewhere, or to throw it in the ocean are not only harmful to the environment, they're illegal, and subject to fines and prison time. You need to find a decompose-able method or a different spell.

TAMPERING WITH SOMEONE'S FOOD OR DRINK –
     No matter what your intentions are, giving someone a love potion or something for their benefit, this is illegal in every state. Not to mention, you don't know if they're allergic to what you put in.

HUMAN SACRIFICE –
     I'm not even going to explain this. You should know better.

IMPROPER DISPOSAL OF SPELL REMAINS –
     Be very careful on how you dispose of a spell, and make sure you aren't introducing mercury or other toxic chemicals into the ecosystem. It's bad for your surroundings, and it's illegal.

ANIMAL ABUSE –
     It does not matter how sacred animal sacrifice and abuse it to your craft, if it breaks the laws, you should rethink it.

TRESPASSING –
     No matter how much you may want to pick some herbs that grow on someone else's property, doing so without permission is trespassing and stealing. Not to

mention dangerous, as there are states with laws that allow the owner to bare arms against trespassers.

FIRE SAFETY –

So you go out into the woods to set up a ritual, cool. but you don't pay attention to the fire alert that day and a stray spark from your ritual candles could start a forest fire and endanger countless people. It does not matter what stars are in position, if Smokey the Bear says no, do it a different day.

This is not about dictating your beliefs or repressing your religious freedom. This is about public safety and respecting other people's rights. Practicing magic does not put you above the law, and it does not make your whims more important than the safety and rights of other people. If you do any of these, you're not expressing your beliefs, you're putting those around you in danger.

Quick Note on Fire Safety

STANDARD PREP:

❖ Tie any hair back! Hair burns very quickly.
❖ Wear non-dangly attire. Pull/tie back any droopy sleeves or similar. You need a clear view of the fire and to not put yourself in danger by being near it.
❖ Something to douse matches in immediately, like a cup of water. Don't set blown-out matches down on flammable surfaces.
❖ Vents! If you're inside and lighting the equivalent to birthday candles, ventilation is not as large an issue, and sometimes can cause larger issues. However, burning large items it best done outside in a fire pit of sorts. Do not burn chemicals, plastics, or unknown mixtures inside.
❖ Dousing method: water, sand, appropriate level fire extinguisher.
❖ Contain the fire in a sandpit, rock circle, metal plate, etc. the immediate area needs to be non-flammable.

THINGS TO NOTE:

Little sparks that carry outside due to the wind are not an issue outside. That being said, they would be a bigger issue inside. So while ventilation is important, you don't want to have wind spreading the fire, or sending things into the flame.

Avoid burning oils if you have little fire experience, as putting an oil-based fire out with water will not put it out, but make it worse.

If you are not confident in your ability to react and put out or handle a fire, please do not light any. Please find a fire alternative for your spells, such as fire elementals like pepper, carnelian, red ink.

Self-Care for the Witch

When one's health is compromised, it's not unusual to want to turn towards magic to aid healing. but not matter how much lavender and rose quartz is in your pockets, or the endless amounts of chamomile incense you burn, it's important to note that magic cannot be used to fix everything when you're feeling poorly, physically, mentally, emotionally, etc. sometimes the best you can do for yourself is exercise a little old fashioned self-care.

HYDRATE—

There is no potion like water. You don't need to force yourself to get the ideal 8 large glasses of water a day, but drinking some when you're feeling poorly is important, especially if you're sick.

EAT—

Everyone eats. Everyone needs food. Something healthy is best, but truly whatever is easiest on your stomach and available to you is just fine. So find something to eat, if only for the spell ingredients you can use after (orange peels, apple rinds/seeds, etc).

MEDS –

Can't work their magic if you don't take them! If a doctor has prescribed you meds, it is important that you take them at the prescribed interval.

RIP –

Take a moment to sort the thoughts that haunt you, put them to ease. Worrying over and lingering on unpleasant things doesn't help, but talking them through with someone to form a plan or rationalize those feelings can help ease them.

SLEEP –

Charge in the moonlight like your crystals. Your crystals get to recharge, so should you! All-nighters are over-glorified of late, but going too long without sleep is hard on your body, and your mind.

SHOWER –

Wash yesterday's dirt away, make room for tomorrow's dirt! A shower can help with your mindset, it can help with a cold, soothe sore muscles, or just leave you feeling better overall.

CLEAN –

A clean space can help keep the cobwebs from your mind. Clutter and a dirty environment affects you mentally in ways you don't realize. Cleansing spirits and bad energies is good for your craft, but cleaning up is still important.

REACH OUT –

A familiar's touch will soothe, but so will getting in contact with friends. While contacting spirits is a great exercise, it is not a replacement for your friends.

If nothing seems to help, reach out to a doctor, therapist, etc. Professional help should never be replaced by magic. Self-care is not a substitute for large pains or dire problems either!

Separating Medicine and Witchcraft

There are bits of history and stories that suggest and note that witchcraft was often interchangeable with medicine during less advanced parts of history. However, now it simply isn't so.

While herbal remedies can be useful and can even be incorporated into your craft, please do not use it or magic to replace common sense.

The appeal to try to use magic to help yourself heal or recover from something may be tempting, but truthfully, there is no magic that will ever be as potent or successful as proven medicines and the knowledge of a trained professional.

Magic can often be hit or miss with their results, and the results are also often, hit or miss in regards to what you actually wanted to happen. For as much science you can involve in your craft, witchcraft is not a science. So until either it becomes one or becomes a lot more accurate, it is more sensible to separate it from health issues.

A good witch can cast a spell. A wise one know when not to.

Herbalism and the Witch

Unfortunately, the temptation for magic to provide an answer is so strong that some turn to herbalism, under the impression it is a branch of magic. It is not.

Herbalism is a diluted science at best. The chemicals inside the herbs, concoctions, and salves that an herbalist will give you are the same as the ones a doctor will recommend, only a doctor will be able to prescribe a more accurate dosage for you problems and is likely better versed in the needed material than your local herbalist.

It is often tempting to try one's own amateur herbal remedies, and there are a number of safety issues with this:

❖ Herbs expire. They can go bad and end up giving a different, if not opposite effect of what you were originally aiming for.

❖ The concentration of the various chemicals can change from one crop to another, and consequently two similar dosages can have entirely different levels of effectiveness.

❖ Concoctions go bad, and often do not come with expiration dates because herbal remedies are not FDA regulated.

❖ There are a number of herbs that we deal with every day in our foods that we do not consider their impacts on our health because we do not take large enough quantities to have a notable reaction. However, simple things like parsley and rosemary, in a concentration or a tincture, would have terrible effects on someone's body, especially if they are pregnant.

❖ Herbs can often conflict with medications you are taking and unless you have the proper training, you or your herbalist would not be able to predict how bad that remedy would be for you.

People often like to go to herbal healers in place of doctors, and while that shouldn't be their only source of medical opinions, however that is their choice.

However, what you must understand is that not every witch is an herbalist.

Like tarot, not every witch you meet is going to be an herbalist, herbal healer, etc. Not every witch reads tarot cards. But the missing detail here is that with herbal remedies there is a lot more room for error than misreading a card.

Being a witch does not give someone an automatic degree in botany, and it certainly doesn't make them a doctor. Lots of witches deal with herbs, yes, but those are most often garden plants and kitchen spices. Even very experienced witches are warned off from handling herbs from mug-wort to belladonna because of their high-risk nature.

A witch can easily give you a spell involving some herbs, but that doesn't mean any of those herbs is going to cure your condition. A witch doesn't necessarily know the medicinal qualities of the herbs they're using, more often just the magical correspondences. This isn't even touching on the fact it's bad to go to a witch for medical problems in the first place, as referenced before. Without a proper knowledge of the herbs they can worsen your condition, especially if they don't know to tell you not to take an herbal-concentrated does of rosemary when you're pregnant, or various other herbs with various conditions/medications.

Chances are, a witch knows just as little as you when it comes to "what can I use for my skin condition? What's good for a sore throat?". Hell, knowing what plants are good for isn't even enough when working with herbs, the room for error after that is so vast.

Tarot and Pendulums Can Get It Wrong

Tarot does not have a degree in law, pendulums are not a doctor. They are estimations based on a situation, and they have the ability to be interpreted differently than the answer we think we receive.

Pendulums, at least for me, have always represented an answered that averages a question down to a yes or no. However, life is rarely that simple. There are almost always other factors. Pendulums don't communicate as simply as we do. "Does Tommy like me?" Well, he doesn't hate you. Maybe he even likes you as a person. But maybe not romantically, and pendulums don't have that nuanced understanding of "like" that we do. "Does Tommy want to romance me?" Maybe, but it could totally be for a practical joke because Tommy is also an asshole.

Tarot tells you your future supposedly, and you ask it medical questions. However, it is in part working off your own knowledge of what is going on. You may have an unknown condition, and it's not going to tell you about it, it's going to tell you how you're going to live and react to things while not knowing. How can tarot tell you that you've got *onychocryptosis* if you've never heard of it? Besides, tarot works solely with themes, not multi-syllabic disease names. You'd have better luck divining what's wrong with you via bibliomancy and a medical text book (don't do that, seriously).

In short, do the tarot reading after you visit the doctor, ask it things it will be able to answer. Tarot is not so much a tool for telling the future as it is telling you about yourself. Pendulums not an exact answer, they are a shrug and "it's kinda leaning towards yes? idk man". They are not exact answers, they're vague advice as best. It's foolish to treat them as cosmic instructions or divine orders.

Simple Potions

Coffee Magic

This is a compiled list of easy correspondences for witchcraft on the run! Or, to start your mornings with a simple potion, ingredients/flavors you can add to your coffee to have a magic start to your day.

SUGAR—
Love and attraction, positive attention

CREAM—
Nurturing, prosperity, and protection

CARAMEL—
Love, kindness, domestic works

CINNAMON—
Divination, fortune, power, prosperity, protection, psychic abilities, spirituality, wealth, and wisdom.

ALMONDS—
Prosperity, wealth, and wisdom

PUMPKINS—
Banishment, divination, healing, prosperity, and protection

BLUEBERRY—
Protection

CHOCOLATE—
Love, lust, health, prosperity and money
VANILLA—
Happiness, love, and lust

HAZELNUT—
Fertility, protection against evil, creativity, intuition, and psychic abilities

RASPBERRY—
Love and protection

Hot Chocolate Magic

There are a lot of subtle ways to work a little magic into your mug! A compiled list of easy recipes to have some magic in your day. For all recipes, melt chocolate, and mix in heated milk slowly.

CARAMEL
½ cup milk, 5 oz. chopped milk chocolate, 3 tsps. caramel, ¼ cup heavy cream. *For love, kindness, domestic works*

CINNAMON SPICE
1 cup milk, 5 oz. chopped dark chocolate, ¼ tsp cinnamon, a pinch cayenne pepper. *For divination, fortune, healing, power, prosperity, protection, psychic abilities, spirituality, wealth, and wisdom.*

ORANGE
1 cup milk, 2 oz. chopped dark chocolate, ½ tbsp. sugar, ½ tbsp. grated orange peel. *For beauty, divination, fortune, love, purification, and wealth.*

WHITE LAVENDER
1 cup whole milk, ½ chopped white chocolate, ¼ tsp lavender flowers. *For chastity, happiness, love, peace, protection, and purification.*

PEPPERMINT
1 cup whole milk, ½ cup chopped milk chocolate, 1 peppermint candy. *For healing, love, psychic abilities, and purification.*

PUMPKIN SPICE

1 cup whole milk, 1 tsp. chocolate powder, ½ tsp pumpkin spice, 1 tsp. maple syrup. *For banishment, divination, healing, prosperity, and protection*

HAZELNUT
1 cup whole milk, a pinch salt, 1 tsp cocoa, 2 tbsp. Nutella or ¼ tsp hazelnut extract. *For fertility, protection against evil, creativity, intuition, and psychic abilities*

VANILLA
½ cup milk, 5 oz. chopped milk chocolate, 1 tsp vanilla extract. *For happiness, love, and lust.*

PEANUT BUTTER
1 cup skim milk, 2 oz. chopped dark chocolate, ¼ cup peanut butter, add cream to taste. *For wealth, love, and fortune.*

Infused Water Magic

Perhaps it's a bit too warm for coffee potions, or hot chocolate magic, or even tea spells, but you still want to work a little magic into your day. Infused waters! Here's *just a couple of suggestions* with fruit and even herbs, and their correspondences. You can even create your own.

For all recipes, chop, cube, or slice all fresh ingredients. Let them sit in a bottle of cool water for a few hours. The longer it waits, the more flavor infuses. Afterwards, you can eat the fruit or infuse it again!

HONEYDEW MELON AND RASPBERRY
For fertility, beauty, abundance, and lunar magic

STRAWBERRY, LIME, AND CUCUMBER
For love, chastity, fertility, healing, fortune, peace and protection.

RASPBERRY, ROSE PETAL, AND VANILLA
For love, protection, divination, healing, psychic abilities. Happiness, and lust.

CITRUS AND CUCUMBER
For purification, protection, beauty, divination, purification, and wealth.

ROSEMARY AND GRAPEFRUIT
For exorcism, healing, love, lust, protection, purification, spirituality and energy

WATERMELON AND MINT
For purification, new beginnings, exorcism, healing, protection, and wealth.

STRAWBERRY, LEMON, AND BASIL
For courage, exorcism, protection, friendship, purification and love.

ORANGE AND BLUEBERRY
For protection, beauty, divination, fortune, love, purification, and wealth

Tea Magic

From the various magical ingredients it includes and the many herbal remedies, tea is often a staple in witchcraft. I've included it because roses, from the actual flower, the petals, the hips, to the fruits it is related to, can be used in a number of things

There are plenty of ways to work to work a little magic into your day without doing a full on ritual, and your daily (hourly?) tea is one of them! Here's *just a couple of suggestions* with fruit, flowers, herbs, and their correspondences.

General Tea Magic

Most teas fall under a few categories: tea plant, floral, fruit and herbal. Teas can be considered type of potion called an infusion. Various types of teas have different steeping times and water temperatures, but you can always chill them and drink them cold too! Most teas have some form of the tea plant in them mixed with other ingredients, but herbal teas do not.

Teas like white, green, oolong, and black tea come from the same plant "Camellia sinensis", and the flavors/properties depend on how the leaves have aged/fermented. These are listed in the amount of least ➡ most fermentation.

WHITE TEA –
Air magic, purification, protection, clarity, realization, meditation, cleansing

GREEN TEA –
Fire magic, healing, love, catalysts, mindfulness, passion, sexual health and new energies

OOLONG TEA –
Water magic, wisdom, reflection and deep concentration, beauty and emotional connections

BLACK TEA –
Strength, stability, endings, finished business, and banishment, expelling negativity.

Herbal Tea Magic

MINT –
> For exorcism, healing, love, lust, protection, and wealth

PEPPERMINT –
> For healing, love, psychic abilities, and purification.

SPEARMINT –
> For healing and love.

GINGER –
> For beauty, love, power, success, and wealth.

FENNEL –
> For healing, protection, and purification.

LICORICE –
> For fidelity, love, and lust.

CINNAMON –
> For divination, fortune, healing, power, prosperity, protection, psychic abilities, spirituality, wealth, and wisdom.

NETTLE –
> For exorcism, healing, lust, and protection.

VANILLA –
> For happiness, love, and lust.

ANISE –
> For, lust, protection, sleep, blessings, youth.

LEMON BALM –
> For healing, compassion, endings, fertility, happiness, healing, love, mental, psychic, success, and youth.

ROSEMARY –
> For exorcism, healing, love, lust, protection, and purification.

SAGE –
  For protection, cleansing, and wisdom.

THYME –
  For courage, healing, love, psychic abilities, and purification.

  There are various blends of herbals teas, as well as with fruits and flowers, though often herbs can be steeped by themselves. What is known as chai tea, is traditional black tea mixed with cardamom, cinnamon and black pepper.

Floral Tea Magic

CHAMOMILE –
  For banishment, love, purification, sleep, and wealth.

DANDELION ROOT –
  For divination and wishes.

HIBISCUS –
  For divination, love, and lust.

PEACH BLOSSOM –
  For fertility, good wishes, longevity, protection, wisdom

JASMINE –
  For love and wealth.

ROSE –
  For divination, fortune, healing, love, protection, and psychic abilities.

ELDERFLOWER –

For joy, protection, prosperity, health and psychic awareness

LAVENDER –
For chastity, happiness, love, peace, protection, and purification.

MARJORAM –
For happiness, healing, love, protection, and wealth.

Of course, this is not to say you should go out and start picking flowers for your tea! Telling plants apart can sometime take an experienced, discerning eye, and it would be unfortunate if anyone tried to make tea with something like poison ivy or poison oak. Unless you have knowledge in this area, it may be best to stick by store-bought teas, which are just as magical as fresh picked flowers/herbs.

Fruit Tea Magic

RASPBERRY –
For love, strength, endurance and reliability.

BLACK CURRANT –
For abundance, lust, and fertility

RHUBARB –
For fidelity and protection.

MANGO –
For harmony, balance, contentment, fertility.

STRAWBERRY –
For fortune, friendship, and love.

LEMON –
For friendship, love, and purification.

CHERRY –
For divination and love.

BLUEBERRY –
For protection.

APPLE –
For banishment, fertility, healing, love, protection, and purification.

PEAR –
For wealth, love and lust.

ORANGE –
For beauty, divination, fortune, love, purification, and wealth.

CRANBERRY –
For protection, positive energy, courage, passion, determination, goals, and action

ROSE-HIP –
For luck, love, and spirituality.

POMEGRANATE –
For divination, luck, wishes, wealth, and fertility

There are a number of combinations of fruit teas, with other types of fruit as well as spices, herbs, flowers and teas.

Tea Blend Potion Recipes

Truth-Spilling Tea

A potion-drink to encourage someone to tell the truth when you share the drink with them, or to inspire truth to come to you in your future. Recipe is for 1 cup of tea.

❖ heat cup of water
❖ add 1.5 tsp dried rosemary needles
❖ Steep for 5 minutes
❖ Strain rosemary needles out
❖ Add the violet as a garnish.
❖ If you are afraid of the truth but still wish to hear it, add honey to the tea so that the words will be sweetened.

Luck tea

A potion-drink to bring you luck. Gather: 2 cup milk (or milk substitutes) 1 tsp dried turmeric, 1 tsp dried ginger, a pinch of pepper, honey to taste.

❖ Heat the milk on medium heat
❖ Add spices
❖ Stir frequently until it simmers. Don't let it reach a boil.
❖ Turn off the heat. Cover and let sit for 10 minutes.
❖ Consume warm. Add honey

Love inspiring Tea

A potion-drink to bring you self-love or strengthen love with another.

- ❖ 1 rose bud
- ❖ 1 tsp. orange extract
- ❖ 1 cup black tea
- ❖ 1 tbsp. black pepper
- ❖ dried orange slices
- ❖ cinnamon to taste
- ❖ cardamom to taste
- ❖ steep 3-5 minutes

Storm Magic

How Do You Collect Dew?

Very, very patiently.

It's not as easy as collecting rainwater, because it requires a lot more work than leaving a bowl out during a storm. First off, start with a jar or something with a wide brim. That way you have a lot of room to catch it, and it'll be less likely to just roll down the outside edges.

Dew is easiest to collect from when it's about to fall off or when it puddles on the leaves. However, those adorable, tiny balled up droplets, are usually nigh-impossible to actually get in the jar.

Most of it I get from where it pools on leaves (hydrangea are very good for this). Put the tip of the leaf into the jar, and then tilt the leaf down, be careful not to disturb it, dew falls very easily. If you work from the top of the plant, the lower leaves catch a lot of the dew you drop or shake loose.

A little bit of science here: since water is what we call a "sticky" molecule, if you wet the inside of the jar and keep the outside dry, it's more likely to go inside the jar.

Chemically, dew/rain is just water and trace atmospheric elements/pollution (so I'd say **do not drink** in large amounts regardless, but especially if you live in a pollution-heavy area, make sure to test the acidity of your rain before touching/handling it.)

Rain water, as a general rule, should not be consumed if it has not gone through proper treatment, filtering, and cleaning.

Rain Divination

A simple divination technique for when you're watching rain drip down the window.

YES/NO DIVINATION

Choose two raindrops near the top of the windows. One is "yes", the other is "no". Meditate on your question.

Whichever merges with another raindrop or reaches the bottom first is your answer.

INTERPRETIVE DIVINATION

Wait for a droplet that catches your attention. it will represent whoever you are inquiring about.

Keep watch for the shapes merged droplets take, it will symbolize an event the occurs because of your interaction with the person

Interpret shapes based on your own associations, or those similar to tea readings

Merged droplets' paths indicate meeting someone new who will have influence on your life

Stray droplets that start in the middle indicate an event within reach but not currently on your path

When the droplets reach the bottom of the windows, that is the unknown, there have yet to be decisions that affect that far into the future.

Seasonal Magic

Spring Witchcraft

MUSHROOMS—
Often indicators of a fairy ring/realm, and though they shouldn't be disturbed, they can be portals for fae work.

INFUSED WATERS—
Not a time for hot drinks, a subtle way to work magic into your day.

WILD FRUIT—
While it isn't advised to eat them, they can be used as offerings to fae, gods, or used in spells.

CLOUDY WEATHER—
Clouds and rain can be used for divination, but also spells of all kinds. A bit of rainwater is a powerful ingredient in any spell or ritual.

HERB/FLORAL BUNDLES—
Herbs are growing, it's a good time to ready bundles of them to dry for the rest of the year.

FLOWER CROWNS—
You can make flower crowns according to each flower's meaning and correspondences, and use their charms.

NEW GROWTH—
Planting herb gardens or all

WARMER WEATHER—
As the season changes over, it's a good time for rituals and spells for shaking off the old and making way for the new.

Summer Witchcraft

ICE CREAM—
From vanilla to strawberry or pecan, your ice cream cone could be used for magical correspondences as well as a sweet treat.

FOOTPRINTS—
In the dirt, the mud, or the sand can be used with footprints for spells that happen over time.

SUN MAGIC—
With the sun being out so much, it too can be used for spells

FIREWORK SPELLS—
Fireworks can be used in spells, but also the energy and wonder they give off.

SEA SHELLS—
Sea shells can be collected for spells

FLOWERS—
Flowers sprouting up everywhere from common clover to roses and sunflowers, are all around, and easy to access for spells.

OCEAN MAGIC—
Beach and sand magic have a number of uses, from grounding and charging to everyday work.

Autumnal Witchcraft

LEAVES —
Good for cleansing negativity and making wishes. In general this is a good time to get in touch with nature, by raking leaves and gardening.

STARGAZING—

There are often stargazing functions done in the fall, at schools and such, and astronomical events happening too!

HAY/STRAW—
There's plenty of this around in this season, and it's good for making a besom/broom, a valuable tool for energy work and banishing bad energies

PUMPKINS —
There's an abundance of pumpkins in the fall, for discreet witches that need materials! Used for, banishment, divination, healing, prosperity, and protection, you can use their materials or carve sigils into them. Or spices the inside and light the candle inside for discreet spells!

RAIN—
With autumn comes hurricane season, and is an excellent time for rain witchcraft, with activities like collecting storm water, or rain divination

BONFIRES—
Good for burning offerings and celebrating pagan holidays, if you wanted to organize one yourself that wouldn't be unheard of. When it's colder, fireplaces are a good substitute

HOT CHOCOLATE—
Good for spells involving love, lust, health, prosperity and money, this treat is an easy way to make a pick-me-up potion.

COFFEE—
The grounds are good for cleansing and banishing and growth, and by adding a pinch of herbs to it, you've got a daily potion on your way to work! (Cinnamon is good for love, vanilla for happiness, etc.)

SPIRITUAL ACTIVITY—
In many cultures, autumn is a time where the veil between earth and spirits weakens, and spirits are more free to walk among us. Try a little spirit work if you dare!

APPLES—
Apples represent the heart, are good for love spells and curses. They are also a good container for burying spells in, because they decompose, unlike glass jars.

ORANGES—
For divination, luck, and cleansing. Also good for burying things in, and you can make a candle out of them.

MUSHROOMS—
Mushrooms are often indicators of a fairy ring/realm, however some witches even use them to aid with divination

CHESTNUTS / ACORNS—
Good for love spells / fertility and protection, but also a sign of the oncoming winter. Bury a handful to ensure prosperity for the next season

CANDY—
With Halloween coming up, there's a lot of candy around. Though it may not be as mystical as using herbs, your candy bin can have its own correspondences.

Winter Witchcraft

HOT COCOA / COFFEE—
Coffee grounds are good for cleansing and banishing and growth. But a cup of either hot drink can double as an easy potion on your way to work.

NATURAL DECOR—
Between wreaths and popcorn strings, there's a lot of natural decor that isn't always readily available most of the year. Making spiced pomander balls is a nice subtle spell for attraction, exorcism, love, protection, and wealth.

PRESENTS—

For many cultures, this is a time of gift-giving. Buying things online or irl for your craft is easier because all you have to do is answer "it's a secret!", and people assume it is a present for the holiday.

SNOW MEN—
Playing in the snow never gets old, and neither does building snowmen. However, with a few herbs packed inside, you've got an easy poppet or a spell that takes action as the snow melts.

ROASTED CHESTNUTS—
Especially if you live in New York, roasted chestnuts are suddenly very popular. They make great offerings if you don't want to eat them, or can be used in spells. Good for love spells / fertility and protection, but also a sign of the oncoming winter. Bury a handful to ensure prosperity for the next season

DRINKING—
Like all times of festivities, there's usually some alcohol involved. During this time of year if can be easier to excuse an offering as a forgotten drink. (Please don't drink if you're underage or it conflicts with your meds)

SEASONAL SPIRIT—
Sometimes during this time of the year you can just feel the magic in the air, whether or not it's actually magic or season's cheer, honoring the seasonal spirit is an option

CHARITY—
This is the time of year charities receive the most, but also go out to call for donations. if you worship/religion calls for acts as well as prayers, this is an easy time to go out volunteer at a soup kitchen, a can drive, or in general donate.

BELLS RINGING—
One prominent type of decor, or at least sound you'll hear a lot this season, is bell ringing. if you wish to use bell ringing to help cleanse an area, this is the season to do it without bringing attention to oneself.

COOKIES—
    Baking cookies is almost traditional this time of year, and if you coordinate the ingredients for a spell, or whoever you leave them out as an offer to, well that's your business.

GENERAL DECOR—
    It is less suspect if you want to decorate for yule with red and green, because in the mainstream understanding it is almost interchangeable with Christmas

BONFIRES AND FIREPLACES—
    Good for burning offerings and celebrating pagan holidays, especially the notion of burning a yule log would not be very unusual to suggest. Take precaution to have a well ventilated area and to not breathe in the smoke
SNOW / ICE / HAIL—
    Like storm water and sea water have their purposes in magic, so do the various types of winter precipitation, and they can be used in many spells. Snow can be for peace or destruction, ice for beauty and offense, and hail in curses.

YULE GOAT—
    Nowadays perceived as a mere Christmas ornament, the making of a yule goat out of straw is believed to be a devotional activity to Thor.

YULE BOAR—
    If you do indulge in eating meat, another subtle way to celebrate yule if through the concept of the "yule boar", eaten to represent fertility.

LIGHTS EVERYWHERE—
    For the witch that has a hard time procuring and lighting candles, this time of year candles are lit more often and with less questions. However, every string of lights can double as candle lights if you need them too.

Grounding Methods

Storm Grounding

To be done during a storm.

Stay in a safe place when you practice this form of grounding. Only allow yourself to get wet if your health allows, and please avoid places that would get you struck by lightning. Have a view/hearing of the rain to the best of your ability

VISUALIZE:

* Each thunder strike rattles you to the core, and leaves nothing there. Each drop of water brings energy that replenishes and re-energizes you.
* Every drop is one of millions, but every drop has importance. Each one soaks into you, cold and bright. It fills you.
* Every sound of every drops rebuilds you from the inside out.
* Each lightning bolt ignites within you, calling up new energies and instilling a calm in its wake.

When you are ready, let the storm fade its hold on you. You are not severing the ties harshly, only letting them fall away, the way rain dissipates and the storm calms down.

Star Grounding

It may seem a bit contradictory to ground with something in the sky rather than the earth. The focus is to ground as if you were a star in space, and to find the power and stability in yourself.

(To the best of your ability) find a view of the clear sky in the sky, and rest somewhere the starlight can reach you

If there is a specific star or constellation you want to draw energy from, have a clear view of it.

VISUALIZE:

❖ Every flare of light over your skin fills you and reacts, igniting power and new energy. It solidifies in your spirit and makes you feel whole.
❖ You are significant, you have your own gravity. Perhaps not the whole universe, but there are things that revolve around you.
❖ You ground within yourself. Old energies burn off and dissipate into the cosmos.
❖ The light that over you brings new, fresh energy. it fills you with the bright and warm

When you are ready, let the star light fade its hold on you. You are not severing the ties harshly, only letting them fall away, and release.

Sea Grounding

Prepare yourself with appropriate sunblock measures! (To the best of your ability) stand barefooted on the beach where the waves can reach and recede from you.

VISUALIZE:

❖ Every wave over your feet pulls you closer to the center of the earth, burying you.
❖ You are becoming part of the earth.

- ❖ Push your old energies out, let the sand exfoliate them from you
- ❖ The water that washes over you brings new, fresh energy. It soaks into you with the cold and the wet

When you are ready, step away from the water gently. You are not severing the ties harshly, only letting them fall away, the way the tide releases you

Moon Grounding

The focus is to ground as if you were an object in space, and to find the stability in yourself. If this strange to conceptualize, astral travel to the moon and use its surface to ground.

(To the best of your ability) find a view of the moon in the sky, and rest somewhere its glow can reach you

Do this during a moon phase that represents the energies you want to draw into yourself.

VISUALIZE:

- ❖ Every flicker of light over your skin fills you and becomes tangible within you. It solidifies in your spirit and makes you feel whole.
- ❖ You are becoming your own moon. You feel the earth's gravity pulling your negative energy away from you. Push your old energies out.
- ❖ The light that washes over you brings new, fresh energy. It illuminates you from the inside out.

When you are ready, let the moonlight fade its hold on you. You are not severing the ties harshly, only letting them fall away, the way the phases turn over and release the earth, it releases you

Spells

Babylon Candle

A spell to get you from one place to another, in your life/mindset or in a more geographic sense

"How many miles to Babylon?
Three score and ten.
Can I get there by candle-light?
Yes, and back again.
If your heels are nimble and light,
You may get there by candle-light."

Gather: kelp, fig, mint, anise, orchid root or pennyroyal. Amethyst or malachite

It's alright if you can't gather all of the herbs/stones, or need to replace some.

Dress the black candle with the herbs.

Embed the stones in the candle's side.

If you have a location/state of mind you want to get to, write it on paper and wrap around the candle.

Light it in a place you want to come back to often, or a place you want to leave.

Rose Quartz Healing Tears

A spell to help heal what is hurt (emotionally).
Gather: full moon water, a piece of rose quartz, pink salt, and lemon balm.
Mix the pink salt and lemon balm into the moon water. Let it soak.

Dip the rose quartz into the water

Let the water from the wet rose quartz drip onto your skin, like tears.

Let it work. Let it out. Things often hurt before they can heal.

Spell to Help Break Bad Habits

A spell that mixes mundane methods with magic to help break bad habits.

Gather: black thread, bay leaf, and a different, healthy habit you want to replace it with.

Identify what brings the habit on: boredom, convenience, etc.

Bind it with the black thread.

Burn the bay leaf and sprinkle the ashes over the new habit

Keep the objects near one another, to remind you to opt for the good habit over the bad one

Radio Voice Sleeping Charm

Gather: an audio playing device, lavender, lemon balm, chamomile tea leaves, a white candle

Light the white candle first. Work around it.

Queue a playlist on the device of either music, talk radio, or podcasts

Sprinkle the chamomile, lemon balm, and lavender around the device.

Chant, "goodnight listeners"

Blow the candle out

Sleep tight.

Plutonic Protection Spell

A spell for the aid of the power of Hades and Cerberus, to protect either oneself or an object. Hellenic / celestial magic fusion.

Gather: sign of Pluto, smoky quartz and representative object of what you wish to protect, a box.

Beseech hades and ask for permission. Do not complete the spell without it.

Respectfully ask hades to take what is to be protected into his territory.

Respectfully ask Cerberus to guard it.

Place the object into the box, attach the sign of Pluto to it.

Invoke the constellation Cerberus and Pluto, for protection.

Seal the box with the smoky quartz inside.

Leave dog treats out to thank Cerberus for his assistance, and an offering for hades thanking him.

Charging With the Sea

Various ways/intents to charge objects with when you are at the shore.

SEA FOAM –
For delicate/love magic.

SANDY WATERS –
Murkiness, best for curses/baneful magic.

SHALLOW, SWEEPING WATERS –
For instilling calm.

BURY IN THE SAND –
Strength, unity.

SEA SALT –
Purification, cleanliness, newness.

ANYWHERE IN THE OCEAN UNDER MOONLIGHT –
The same as charging with moon water or moonlight, with the added power of the ocean/sea

Don't charge stones directly in water if they are known
to react badly to water or salt. Be careful not to lose
anything in the water either

Job Prosperity Spell

Write your name on the bay leaf, sprinkle cardamom
over it. Burn over a green candle. Chant as it burns:

*"Willing to work, but better for a more decent buck
bring a job, by the candle I gather good luck."*

Paper Wish Spell

Know your wish. You can write it plainly or make it a
sigil. Write it on a piece of paper, draw little stars around it.
Gather clover leaves, dill, and cinnamon.
Roll/bundle the herbs up inside, tie with thread.
Burn the bundle on a fire-safe surface.
Chant until it has all burned out:

*"By the powers of clover, dill, and cinnamon
Let these herbs bring my wish to fruition!"*

Save the ashes in a container in case you wish to undo
the wish.

Amethyst Home Spell

A spell to make things feel like home.
Gather: amethyst, basil, sea salt, and thistle.
Sprinkle the windows with sea salt.
Hand a braid of thistle and basil above you door
Place the amethyst under or above your bed.

Love Spells

Unwanted Lover Spell (Love Spell Reversal)

You will need:
- ❖ The pieces/ingredients you used for the original love spell. Salt and burn what you can.
- ❖ A rose, burned to ash
- ❖ Something representative of this guy, a picture perhaps. Burn it to ash.

Mix these things together, then pour out into a little pile of ashes on the front or back step. Chant:

"Get the fuck out of my life
I do not like you
You are causing me strife
Shove off, creep."

Sweep the ashes away into the wind with a broom. (Outdoors would be preferable). Sweep it away into the wind.

Rose Romance Spell

A spell to aid romance for couples that don't connect in all the conventional ways

Gather: a whole peach, rose quartz, a normal rock, and one of the items below that corresponds to what you feel is missing from the relationship.

- ❖ dill = communication
- ❖ vanilla = lust
- ❖ poppy seeds = romance
- ❖ cumin = fidelity
- ❖ coconut = chastity
- ❖ bluebell = trust
- ❖ cypress = peace

Cut the peach in half, take the pit out.

Put the rose quartz and the normal rock where the pit was

Sprinkle your chosen ingredient over the inside of the peach.

Close up the peach.

Bury the peach. Keep the pit.

Stay with Me Spell

Carve the candle with both of your names, one of either side. Tie a string around the candle, and light the orange candle. Chant:

"I tie this knot, with a string, long
to keep our communication strong.
By this candle's orange hue,
I preserve the relation between us two."

Wait until the wax melts over the string. Blow out the candle, and preserve the string in your room.

A Spell to Help Someone See Your Feelings

Write a letter detailing your feelings and roll it up. Optional, add some herbs that correspond with your situation. Seal something inside the letter, something that represents the person, whether it is some of their hair or a picture of them, etc.

Light a blue candle, and wait until the flame burns strong, then chant, burning the letter:

"Know my feelings, and how you have snubbed me
by the blue candle that burns: to this gain clarity."

Blow out the candle.

Long Distance Spell

You will need four things. Two things from you, two things from your friend. Pair one of your things with one of theirs. Tie each pair together with a white thread.

Place them by a white candle, on either side. Sprinkle the candle with thyme, strawberry, and lemon balm. Chant:

"Through hardship and distance
and all other resistance
our bond will not be neglected
we will remain connected
by candle and herb I bless these charms
by them, our bond comes to no harm."

Let the charms charge by the candle, and after the spell is done give your friend the other charm.

Show Me Your Love Spell

Dry some rose petals and crush them, add dill. Put a little in his pillowcase.

Make a little circle out of the rest of the herbs, put the candle in the center. Burn it and chant:

"By rosemary and dill this spell starts
Draw me closer and show your cares
As I've held you in my arms
And you hold me in your heart."

SAVE THE HERBS IN A BAG. If the spell becomes too much, so you can salt and burn them to end it.

Use this spell with caution.

Simple Love Attraction Spell

Carve a heart shape onto the candle. Light the candle, feel it's warmth but be careful not to burn yourself.

Whisper or think:

"As I watch the flame dance
I draw to me hopes of romance.
As it warms my face, I'll warm others hearts,
Who graze the feathers of cupid's dart."

Blow out the candle.

Bubble Your Feelings Spell

A spell to bubble feelings that are causing you harm, such as unrequited love

Gather: a pearl, an object that represents your feelings, a box, and a white candle.

If you do not have a pearl, use clear quartz or glass.

Gather up your feelings and push them onto the object.

Box the object up.

Drip white wax onto the opening of the box, sealing it.

Draw a circle in the air around the box with the pearl.

It is finished. It will not bother you until you unbubble it.

This can be done without an object, only with thought, but it is harder to accomplish them.

Rekindling Spell

First find a box of matches that you'll use. Put a rose petal in the box, or some rose quartz, and leave it overnight under the moonlight to charge with loving energy. If you need to use a lighter instead, leave it in a jacket or pants pocket with the rose petals or quartz, same deal with the moonlight.

Find moment to light a literal fire between you, whether it is a campfire, or maybe you sit down to dinner and decide to have a candlelit meal for once. You can sit across or next to him, as long as you're generally pointed to the candle.

Use the prepared matches/lighter to light the fire. Have a friendly conversation over the fire. Feel the fire's energy filling up your relationship.

Drop the word "spark" into the conversation casually. This is the only word you will need for the incantation, and you only need to say it once. Let the conversation last as long as it can.

Put the fire/candle out safely, but try to keep the fire's energy in mind. It does not go out with the flame if you don't let it.You can do this spell more than once if you like, but try to space it out.

Sweeten Your Feelings Jar Spell

Find a taglock of you and the person, it should be small enough to fit in the jar. Mix the honey, sugar, and lemon seeds together in the jar. Optional, light a yellow/orange/pink candle, depending on the nature of the relationship. Put the taglock in the jar, chant:

"Sweet as sugar, by this honeyed spell,
only in nectarous feelings our bond shall dwell
puckered lips, our love shall never be sour,
from these seeds sweeter feelings flower."

Seal with wax (optional).

To dispose/break the spell: rinse the mixture out of the jar, cleanse the taglock and empty jar.

The Smolder" Love Spell

A pocket love spell/glamour you can use by fluttering your eyelashes.

If you wish to enchant a specific mascara or eye shadow, apply the charm to the outside of the makeup container instead of your eyes.

Gather: moon water, rose petals, and strawberry leaves.

Dab around eyes with the clean water, avoid direct contact with eyes.

Dab the water droplets with the rose petals and strawberry leaves.

Apply to your eyes either the day/night of, or by makeup.

Note: use clean water you don't mind washing your face with to make the moon water, wash the rose petals and strawberry leaves.

Friendship Spells

Friendship Fastening Spell

A consensual binding spell for friends, inspired by hand-fasting ceremonies.

This spell is to be done with both parties present.

Gather: strawberry leaves, yellow string, a white candle, and representative objects of each party involved.

Using the yellow string, wrap the representative objects together with the strawberry leaves between them. Take turns wrapping the object with the string.

Chant while wrapping:

"With your hands and mine
through this string we entwine
secure a friendship forever fine."

Seal the knot with white wax.

A Spell to Let Emotions/Empathy Flow Between Two People

Cleanse and charge the items you will be using.

If it's in your practice, cast a circle big enough for the two of you to sit across from one another, with two bowls in between, invoke your deities, cleanse, etc.

Best done outside in the grass. Light two blue candles between you.

Take something of hers and something of yours, a ring or a bracelet perhaps. Pour the water into the empath's bowl.

Use water charged under the moon, mix in herbs of thyme, bay leaf, and lemon. Fill your bowl almost to the brim. Cup your hands in the water and chant as you pour the handfuls of water into her bowl, over her hands, sitting in her bowl:

"My bowl overflows,
While yours like a sieve.
What the empath knows
From this night on, I give."

Have her wash her hands in the water accumulating in her bowl.

"I unburden from your mind
the weight of others hearts
Our efforts combined,
I share your knowledge in part."

Repeat the chants until you have emptied half of what you had into her bowl. Blow out the candles, close the circle, thank your gods, etc. Bottle up the water from each bowl and keep it in your rooms.

"When alone and you feel the bond is wearing thin,
repeat the chant and sprinkle a little water over your token."

When together, wear the items at the same time and tell her about the things you feel, and have her respond to these things. End the exchange with this chant:

"Burden no more, when it is shared
Through the bond of us two paired."

Friendship/Conversation Attraction Spell:

Find something that represents yourself, preferably small.

Eat some strawberries while you say this chant:

"With friendship on my mouth, I know
I attract friends and conversation
these seeds I plant, discourse I sow
this spell will draw my friendship's foundation."

Save some of the seeds, place them, the object that represents you, and some rosemary in an envelope/sachet. Keep it in your pocket for when you are in the same area as the people you want to be friends with.

Bring Us Closer Spell

Carve the person's name into the candle, and yours on the other side.

Chant:

"With the power of our names
I bring our paths to intertwine
through this burning flame
to learn of you is my design."

Let the candle burn all the way through, or at least until it has burned through both names. Do not leave the candle unattended.

Glamours

Venus Transformation Glamour

A glamour to transform the perceptions of the ordinary to beautiful and powerful

If you want to use a wand or similar tool, feel free.

Gather: almond apricot, holly and daisy.

With each the almond, apricot, and holly trace a circle in the air around yourself, encircling yourself with their power. Wear the daisy in your hair. Go feel pretty and powerful.

Seductive Words Glamour

A lipstick/chapstick glamour to make your words extra convincing/persuasive

Gather: chapstick/lipstick of your choice (though red would work best) moon water, a basil leaf, a spring of rosemary

Soak the basil leaf and sprig of rosemary for an hour in the moon water.

Put a drop of moon water on the lipstick

If you want to make the spell for something/someone specific, add a sigil to the lipstick before you put it on.

Shine Like the Sun:

Perform spell early in the morning, sit before the sun as it rises.

Brush your hair, and burn any strands that come out while brushing it in the candle. Take care not to burn yourself.

"Eyes bright as my laugh and hair to match
by the fierce sun, I keep the light I catch!"

Blow out the candle.

However, some simple mundane alternatives for the hair: spending a lot of time outside in the sunlight has been known to lighten the hair, or using a bit of lemon juice.

Glow Like the Moon

Light your candle, a plain one or a pink one. Do at night, look up at the mostly full moon. Chant:

"Moon, bright and full, grant me your glow
bring back the beauty, that I used to know."

Bask in the moonlight for a little while, until you feel it is done. Blow out your candle.

Protection Spells

Pumpkin Wards

Gather: a pumpkin or similar gourd, a carving station, a candle, and a mixture of cloves, nutmeg, coffee grinds, and cinnamon.

Scoop out the pumpkin seeds, save a handful of the seeds.

Carve any face or design you like into the pumpkin, but carve with the intent that it will scare spirits away from your house.

Spice the inside of the pumpkin with the herbs.

Before you light the candle, drop a pumpkin seed on each of the corners of the area you wish to protect.

Anoint the candle with the spices or a sigil if you like.

Light the candle, let it burn safely outside in a non-flammable area.

If you like, you can even carve sigils into the pumpkin if you like, to modify the spell against anything else you want to protect yourself from this night.

Rose Quartz Shielding Spell

A shielding spell that both protect you from nearby people's negativity, and dispels peoples' negativity to a state where they feel loved, safe, and non-combative

Gather: rose quartz, coffee beans, an acorn, and string.

- rose quartz for love and good feelings, healing
- coffee beans for protection and banishing negativity
- acorn for happiness

Craft a charm you can have on your person out of the materials. Charge and cleanse the rose quartz before using, to increase effectiveness.

Bindings

Wrapped Around Your Finger

Take one glove from a pair the person has worn. Write the names of the women he talks to online and write them down, slip them inside each of the fingers of the gloves. Bind each of the fingers with black thread/string. Seal each knot with the wax from a black candle, and after each finger, chant:

"Give me your hands, which you promised to me
I have your voice but it is only lip service.
To exchange messages with girls you won't be free.
By black thread, let this spell preserve us."

Bind it tight as you can with the thread, seal with black thread. Keep in a box out of sight.

Lapis Water Binding

A spell to bind and banish those to a place they cannot travel from.

Gather: lapis lazuli*, sea salt, water, a rock or something heavy, as an anchor, two taglocks, black thread. Create one taglock for the person/thing you are binding.

Create the other taglock, for the part of yourself that has been affected by the person/thing. This is to bind the affect-or and the affected area away together.

Mix the sea salt and the water. Bind the taglocks and the anchor with black thread. Drown the bound objects, chant the above quote if you like.

You can put the lapis lazuli in the water during this enchantment, but know it is a water-soluble stone. Alternatively, you could just hold it over the bowl for the spell.

note, you can replace the lapis lazuli with pumpkin seeds

To Bind A Bully Spell:

Take a picture of her, or an effect of hers, and begin tying it up with black string or thread. Chant:

"I restrict you, you won't bother me
your words won't touch my mind
of this spell you won't be free
until to me you are kind."

Repeat the chant until you have covered the entire thing with the black string/thread, make sure you cannot see any bit of the original object.

Some mundane advice: you don't have to go to her to stop her doing this to you, you can avoid the drama entirely. You can talk to your teachers, your guidance counselors, your and her parents, you can even request to switch to a different class.

Tongue Tying Spell

Find something that represents his mouth, a drawing or a picture, anything. Write the names of the girls you don't want him to talk to on the back. Bind with black thread, and then burn it over a black candle. Chant:

"Your tongue is tied, it belongs to me
I have your voice but it is only lip service.
To flirt with other girls you won't be free.
By black thread and candle, let this spell preserve us."

Keep the ashes in an envelope.

Know What You Have Done Spell

Find a picture of the two of you, and roll it up with some rosemary inside, fresh or dried, whichever is easier to procure. Tie it with string, and light a black or white candle. Burn the rolled picture.

"Wasted friendship, wasted years,
Know and feel these wasted tears.
By broken bond and rosemary
Know, and regret what you have done to me."

Wash That Man Out of Your Hair

A spell to forget what they did to you. Find a bar of soap. It can be plain soap, or soap scented/made with things that are appropriate to your situation.

Carve what he did that you wish to forget into the soap bar. Use the soap bar on the parts specific to what they did. Chant:

"Gone, gone, gone with the suds
popped like bubbles and the soap between
I wash you away with every scrub
I'm free of your memory, I'm squeaky clean."

Use the soap bar until the carving is gone and become all soap suds. Rinse it all off, and envision the suds taking away everything that he has done that you want to forget. As you watch the last of the bubbles go down the drain, say:
"It's it all gone, the memory is down the drain
it is all gone, it will never bother me again."

Communication Spells

Tiny Truth Spell

Write your question and the person's name on the paper. Light the candle, and as you burn it, chant softly:

"Whisper once your word of truth
Just one answer I wish to know
Bring to me through tongue and tooth
I plant the seed and truth I'll sow."

Mental Message Spell

Write the message on a piece of paper, add dill and rosemary if you like when you're done. Roll it up, herbs inside. Tie it up.

"With this note I hope you hear
these heartfelt words I hold so dear
through fire, know my words' intent
with this message I have sent."

Burn the paper.

Stop Ignoring Me Spell

Place a small pinch of dill, and a fragment of a rose petal under your tongue. Concentrate on the intention "open your mouth, open your heart" for a little while. It's okay if you accidentally swallow some, both are edible, but try not to.

Give the person a kiss on the cheek.
Then go into the bathroom alone. Chant/think:

"Open your mouth, let me see your heart
Spill the feelings that are keeping us apart."

As you rinse the herbs out of your mouth with water, imagine their opening up to you.

Repeat if you like, but no more than twice a day.

Contact Spell

If your practice calls for it, invoke your corresponding deities/elements/planets, cast a circle, etc. This is optional.

Draw the sign of mercury and charge it. Place a shallow bowl over the sign, place your phone opposite you, near the bowl.

Write your and the person's number on separate pieces of paper. If you have a piece of clear quartz (preferably cleansed/charged but no big deal if it isn't) rub it over the numbers, three times each, then place it in the bowl. If you have no quartz, use your finger. Chant, say, sing or think:

> *"Any words you have waiting for me,*
> *Be brought to the front of your mind*
> *Please, from me, the powers that be,*
> *Lead my friend, that he should find*
> *Our correspondence is long overdue,*
> *Spark a dialogue, to me from you!"*

After, take the papers and burn them, or tear them up into small pieces. Mix in the bowl, mix in your caraway and dill. Leave by the window, or sprinkle outside in the wind, in the direction of that person's house.

Of course, there is a mundane method as well, simply call or text them yourself. I know that option is scarier, but results are 100% quicker, so I'm going to include a quick little courage spell: take a pinch of basil, hold it to your heart and repeat the things you want to say to the person, until you feel a bit stronger. Place the basil under your tongue, drink some water and text/call them.

Curses

Too Much Attention Hex

Someone bother you? Here's a hex to let them know how it feels to have attention they don't want.

Gather: paper, pen, ylang ylang, black-eyed susans and thread. Take their words, write the things they said down on a strip of paper.

Smear the words with the black eyed susan.

Roll with ylang ylang and wrap with thread.

Burn, or bury.

Thorn in My Side Curse

A curse for those that consistently abuse or hurt you. a spell to turn those that are a "thorn in your side" into a thorny consequence when they try to hurt you

Gather: red candle. A thorn or something sharp, or a representative object of relationship, like something used to hurt you, and a hair from your abuser

Light the candle and tilt it at an angle so the melted wax drips off the candle. Be very careful

Use the wax to encase the hair.

Prick yourself slightly with the thorn, or if the object has been used against you before, no need.

Press the thorn into the wax, and tell it,

"All that you have done to me,
will be rebound onto you."

Hide the ball of wax.

Cerberus Curse

A curse that falls upon those who attempt to hurt something under the *Plutonic Protection Spell*, and sets Cerberus on their ass until they back off.

Often called the "Hound of Hades", is a multi-headed dog, who guards the gates of the underworld

Gather: scale (sequins are a replacement) dog fur (preferably shed while petting one), thorns and the box.

Perform the Plutonic Protection Spell.

Invoke and inscribe the constellation Cerberus on the box

Arrange the thorns like teeth along the opening of the box

Attach the fur to the box

Attach the scale or sequins in a pattern like a tail.

Seal the box and keep in a safe place.

Leave an offering out for Cerberus to thank him for protecting it.

Pumpkin Head Curse

A season curse for banishing and "burning" that you can set whenever you feel the person has wronged you.

Gather: a pumpkin (or a small pumpkin like gourd), a carving knife, a candle/matches, cinnamon, black salt, chili pepper

Carve the pumpkin/gourd in the image/interpretation of the intended target. It does not need to be literally.

Exaggerate the features of how the person has been hurting you.

Spice inside the pumpkin with cinnamon, black salt, and chili pepper

Light candle inside.

Don't burn inside the house.

Dispose of the pumpkin.

The curse only lasts while the candle is lit

Burn Your Wishes Curse

A simple curse to keep someone's wishes from coming true.

Gather: seeded dandelions, matches, burnable area, paper, taglock

You can choose to make a ring of dandelions, or bundle, or simply use one.

Note, the more dandelions the more wishes you destroy.

If you want to target specific wishes, write them down on slips of paper and wrap them around the stems of the dandelion.

Place taglock in the middle of the circle, or around the bundle.

Burn the dandelions.

Dispose of safely. Keep the taglock.

Your Heart in My Hand Curse

When you squeeze the poppet heart they will be plagued by nightmares of what they did to you, and feel a general sense of being lost in life.

Gather a taglock, fabric to make the poppet heart, black or red, a black candle, twigs, dirt, and bugs.

Light the candle. Take the taglock of theirs and make a poppet heart containing it. Fill it with dirt, twigs, and bugs (optional).

Construct and seal the poppet with black candle wax.

'Red in Your Ledger' Curse

A curse to inflict all the pain a person has caused back on them, one item at a time.
Gather: a disposable notebook, red ink, matches, and a taglock.
Write down an itemized list of everything awful the person has done to you, and anyone else you know they have hurt. Fill the book if you must
Bind it with the tag lock inside.
Chant three times:

*"You must know you have debts to pay
and your scorned will collect one day."*

Burn the book.

Endnote:

Witchcraft is often elusive and hard to comprehend, even to those who have not been practicing it for a very long time. Though its essence is fairly simple once one reaches it, witchcraft as a topic has many branches and becomes steadily more complicated as you understanding of it grows.

You are the sole one in charge of your craft. There are many witches out there and coven leaders who may try to tell you that you must follow their traditions, but they are wrong to do so. Only you can decide how to practice your craft, and what creates the magic true to you.

81788136R00057